LET'S WEIGH
THE
EVIDENCE

by Barry D. Burton

Published by Chick Publications
P.O. Box 662, Chino, CA 91710
Printed in the United States of America

INTERNATIONAL DISTRIBUTORS

Christ Is The Answer, Inc.
Box 5167, Station A
Toronto, Ontario, Canada
Phone: (416) 699-7800

Chick Publications Distributor
P.O. Box 35359
Auckland 10
New Zealand

Penfold Book & Bible House
P.O. Box 26
Bicester, Oxon, England OX6 8PB
Tel: 0869-252182

Evangelistic Literature Enterprise
P.O. Box 10
Strathpine, Q'ld., Australia 4500
Phone: (07) 205-7100

DEDICATION

I would like to dedicate this book to Brother George Galligar for his patience, friendship, stability, loyalty and support. Not to forget the many phone calls I made to him, and the many hours I spent talking to him about the different translations, especially the calls waking him up at night.

To . . . Brother George Galligar I dedicate this book. "Hey George, We might get knocked down, but we won't get knocked out!"

Copyright © 1983
By
Barry D. Burton

Library of Congress
Catalog Card No. 83-71271

Eighth Printing

184/E
ISBN: 0-937958-17-4

TABLE OF CONTENTS

INTRODUCTION

The issue of the modern translations is controversial, even in fundamental circles. The issue is *not* one of inspiration, of course. We believe in the inspiration of the Scriptures.

THE BIBLE SAYS:
> *"All scripture is given by inspiration of God, and is profitable for doctrine, for reproof, for correction, for instruction in righteousness."* II Timothy 3:16

The issue is one of preservation. Did God Preserve His Word perfect for us today, or was it only perfect "in the original autographs"? If God has not preserved His Word perfect, but has allowed some errors, then, since we don't have the "original autographs," we must assume that we have been teaching and preaching out of a book that is not completely reliable.

If we believe that the Bible is still perfect, then we must still answer the question, *"Which* Bible is the one that God has preserved for us?" Since the modern translations are different from the King James Bible, not just in wording but in doctrine, and since two conflicting books cannot *both* be perfect, we must make a choice.

We believe that the Bible (KJV) is the Word of God, and we also believe that God has preserved it perfect for us today. It was not just perfect in the original autographs.

> Psalm 12:6-7 says:
> *"The words of the Lord are pure words...*
> *Thou shalt **keep** them, O LORD, thou*
> *shalt **preserve** them from this generation*
> *for ever."*

7

This booklet was written so that born-again, Bible-believing Christians everywhere, may be able to answer these two questions:

1) Do we have the absolutely perfect Word of God today? (The question is NOT, "was it perfect when it was written?" BUT "Is it still perfect?"

2) If we have the inerrant Word of God, *which* Bible is it?

Our prayer is that Christians will be able to . . .

> ". . . *be ready always to give an answer to every man that asketh you a reason of the hope that is in you with meekness and fear.*"
> I Peter 3:15

P.S.
Logic tells us that 2 opposite statements cannot *both* be true. Therefore, two contradicting "Bibles" cannot *both* be the perfect Word of God. If one is true, then the other is false.

CHAPTER ONE

FAITH

HOW ARE WE SAVED?

THE BIBLE SAYS:
"For by grace are ye saved <u>through faith</u>; and that not of yourselves: it is the gift of God: Not of works, lest any man should boast." Ephesians 2:8-9

HOW DO WE GET *FAITH?*

BY THE *WORD OF GOD.*

THE BIBLE SAYS:
"So then faith cometh by hearing, and hearing by the word of God." Rom. 10:17
AND
*"Being born again, not of corruptible seed, but of incorruptible, by the **word of God,** which liveth and abideth for ever."* I Peter 1:23

YOU SEE . . . THE WORD OF GOD IS VITALLY IMPORTANT!!!!!

*"And that from a child thou hast known the **holy scriptures,** which are able to make thee wise unto **salvation** through **faith** which is in Christ Jesus."* II Timothy 3:15

Can we trust it???????
Do we have God's Word today???????
If we do . . . which Bible is God's Word???????

HERE'S HOW IT WORKS . . .

A MAN REALIZES THAT HE IS A SINNER.

THE BIBLE SAYS:

"For all have sinned and come short of the glory of God." Romans 3:23

AND

"Wherefore, as by one man sin entered into the world, and death by sin; and so death passed upon all men, for that all have sinned." Romans 5:12

THEN HE LOOKS INTO "THE BOOK" AND SEES THAT . . .

"For the wages of sin is death; but the gift of God is eternal life through Jesus Christ our Lord." Romans 6:23

"But God commendeth his love toward us, in that, while we were yet sinners, Christ died for us." Romans 5:8

THEN . . . HE LEARNS THE ANSWER . . .

"That if thou shalt confess with thy mouth the Lord Jesus, and shalt believe in thine heart that God hath raised him from dead, thou shalt be saved." Romans 10:9

"Who his own self bare our sins in his own body on the tree, that we, being dead to sins, should live unto righteousness: by whose stripes ye were healed."

I Peter 2:24

10

THE BIBLE ALSO SAYS . . .

". . . and the blood of Jesus Christ his Son cleanseth us from all sin." I John 1:7

"For God so loved the world, that he gave his only begotten Son, that whosoever believeth in him should not perish, but have everlasting life." John 3:16

THEN . when a person becomes a Christian, God calls him a soldier of Jesus Christ . . .

"Thou therefore endure hardness, as a good soldier of Jesus Christ."
II Timothy 2:3

. . . AND gives him armor for protection . . .

*"Above all, taking the **shield of faith,** wherewith ye shall be able to quench all the fiery darts of the wicked."*
Ephesians 6:16

Who throws the fiery darts?_____

What shield do we have? _____

What do we have for a weapon? _____

A SWORD  OR A BUTTER KNIFE?

The Christian's only offensive weapon, is his sword.

*"And take the helmet of salvation, and the **sword** of the Spirit, which is the **word of God.**"* Ephesians 6:17

*"For the **word of God** is quick, and powerful, and sharper than any two edged **sword** . . ."* Hebrews 4:12a

11

NOW . . . The Christian is in a battle with the devil . . .

AND, the devil is out to destroy the Christian's sword.

HOW . . . is he destroying the *Word of God*?????????????

    1) Through *DOUBT* and *CONFUSION*
    2) *By changing* the Bible and *omitting* words, verses
       and paragraphs of God's Word.

WHAT . . . is he using to do this?????????????

      ✱ THE MODERN VERSIONS OF THE BIBLE! ✱

 **I HAVE SOME QUESTIONS.**

"What are you trying to say? Are you saying that some books that are called 'Bibles' are not really the Bible at all?"

    "YES"

"Are you trying to say that there are really 'counterfeit' Bibles being sold today?"

    "YES"

(Don't get mad yet, you still have a lot more to read . . .
            then you can get mad.)

"ARE YOU SAYING THAT THE PEOPLE THAT READ THESE "OTHER" BIBLES ARE BAD PEOPLE?"

    "NO" - most people haven't compared the new Bibles enough to realize that there really is a **BIG** difference.

"WHAT BIBLE DO YOU THINK IS THE REAL WORD OF GOD?"

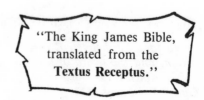

"The King James Bible, translated from the **Textus Receptus**."

"IS THERE REALLY AN **IMPORTANT** DIFFERENCE, OR IS IT JUST A DIFFERENCE IN UPDATING OLD LANGUAGE?"

"It's an **important** difference!" - It would be one thing if they just changed a few old-fashioned words . . . but the fact is that the **basic doctrines** of the Christian faith are **attacked**!

"WHAT DOCTRINES?"

"The doctrine of the **diety of Christ,** (that Christ is God), the **virgin birth** of Christ, the **infallibility** of the Bible, the doctrine of **salvation** by **faith,** and the **Trinity.**

"ARE THERE ANY OTHER CHANGES?"

"YES" - there are between 5,000 and 36,000 changes depending on which version you are looking at. They take out part of the **Lord's prayer,** change parts of **communion,** leave out the **resurrection** in Mark, **omit** hundreds of words and phrases, and **downgrade** the Lordship of Jesus Christ . . . just to name a few.

"HOW CAN YOU LUMP ALL THE NEW VERSIONS TOGETHER AGAINST THE KING JAMES BIBLE?"

Dr. Gordon D. Fee, a professor at Wheaton College said in an article in the magazine *Christianity Today*...

"The contemporary translations **as a group** have one thing in common: they tend to **agree against** the KJV . . . in omitting hundreds of words, phrases, and verses."

NOTICE . . . Dr. Fee was promoting the new versions yet he realized that the new versions, as a whole, are different.

"**WHY** ARE THEY DIFFERENT?"

"KEEP READING — YOU'LL FIND OUT . . ."

CHAPTER TWO

DOUBT AND CONFUSION

It all started way back in the Garden of Eden.
God commanded Adam:

*"Of every tree of the garden thou mayest freely eat: But of the tree of the knowledge of good and evil, **thou shalt not** eat of it: for in the day that thou eatest thereof thou shalt surely die."*

Gen. 2:16-17

THEN . . .

Satan came to tempt Eve.
HOW DID HE DO IT??????????
By *casting doubt on God's Word*!!!!!
Satan's first 4 words to Eve were . . .

"Yea, hath God said . . . ??

The *first* thing Satan did when talking to Eve was to *cast doubt* on God's Word!!!

AND EVE FELL FOR IT . . .

Satan is doing the exact same thing today. LOOK in your modern versions of the Bible.   On nearly every page they say in the footnotes . . .

"this verse not found in the earliest mss." or

"Later mss. add" or "some authorities say" or

"other ancient authorities omit this verse" or

"other authorities add, some ancient"

What is it? *DOUBT CASTING,* that's what it is! Over 100 times in the New Testament alone, Satan is able to say . . .

"Yea, hath God said this . . .?" "Yea, hath God said that . . .?" "Yea, do you think God said . . .?" "Yea, perhaps God said??" "Yea, maybe God didn't say . . .!"

EVEN WORSE THAN THAT . . . In the front of the New American Standard Version it says . . . "Brackets in the text are around words *probably not* in the original writings."

What did they put in brackets? Mark 16:9-20, 12 verses about the *resurrection* of Christ, Mark 9:44 about *Hell.* Mark 9:46 about *Hell,* Matthew 6:13 the last part of the Lord's prayer, John 7:53-8:11 (12 more verses) and many, many more!!

DO YOU SEE WHAT SATAN IS DOING?
THE BIBLE SAYS:

> *"So then faith cometh by hearing, and hearing by the word of God."*
>
> Romans 10:17

We are saved by *FAITH.* BUT . . . the OPPOSITE OF faith is DOUBT!! Satan is using DOUBT and CONFUSION to try to destroy the Word of God!

THE BIBLE SAYS:

> *"For ever, O LORD, thy word is settled in heaven."* Psalm 119:89
>
> *"Heaven and earth shall pass away, but my words **shall not** pass away."*
>
> Matthew 24:35
>
> *"God is not a man, that he should lie; neither the son of man, that he should repent: **hath he said, and shall he not do it? or hath he spoken, and** shall he not make it good?"* Numbers 23:19

God is NOT a liar! He *has* preserved his Word for us! We don't have to doubt it!!!!

LET'S BE SMARTER THAN EVE WAS!!!!!!!

CONFUSION?

BIBLE STUDY GROUP . . .

"TURN IN YOUR BIBLES TO . . ."

"I CAN'T FIND IT . . .
    IT'S NOT IN *MY* BIBLE . . ."

"*MY* BIBLE SAYS . . ."

"OH, MINE SAYS SOMETHING
    DIFFERENT . . ."

"WELL, MINE SAYS THIS . . ."

"I WONDER WHAT'S RIGHT??????? . . ."

"I DON'T KNOW . . . I'M CONFUSED . . .?.?.?.?.?"

THE BIBLE SAYS:
*"For God is not the author of
confusion,"* I Corinthians 14:33

If God isn't . . . then who is?????????????

CHAPTER THREE

DOCTRINES

THERE IS A DIFFERENCE!

DEFINITION of FUNDAMENTALISM

New Standard Encyclopedia vol. five, page 375

"In United States Protestantism, a conservative movement opposing modernism in the churches. The movement beginning about 1910, opposed liberal attempts to reconcile the teachings of Christianity with the findings of science, especially evolution. The conservatives insisted on five fundamentals:

1) the *inerrancy, infallibility,* and *literal* truth of the Bible in *every* detail;

2) the virgin birth and complete deity of Jesus Christ;

3) the physical resurrection of Christ and all dead;

4) the atoning sacrifice for the sins of the world;

5) and the second coming of Christ in bodily form."

IF YOU DON'T BELIEVE IN ALL FIVE OF THESE "FUNDA-MENTALS" THEN DON'T CALL YOURSELF A FUNDA-MENTALIST!

19

THE MODERN VERSIONS ATTACK THE DOCTRINE OF THE *DEITY OF CHRIST.*

I Timothy 3:16
(King James)
"And *without controversy* great is the mystery of godliness: *God was manifest in the flesh,* justified in the Spirit, seen of angels, preached unto the Gentiles, believed on in the world, received up into glory."

This verse clearly teaches that *Jesus is God!*

NOTICE: "*God* was manifest in the flesh."

Jesus is the one who came in the flesh . . .

THEREFORE . . .   **JESUS IS GOD!!!!!!**

I Timothy 3:16
(New American
Standard, NAS)
"And by common confession great is the mystery of godliness: He who was revealed in the flesh, Was vindicated in the Spirit, Beheld by angels, Proclaimed among the nations, Believed on in the world, Taken up in glory."

Notice the tricky, deceitful, sly, changes . . .

The Bible declares, "*God* was manifest in the flesh"

The NAS CHANGES it to . . . "*He* who was revealed in the flesh, *Was* vindicated in the Spirit . . ."

1) By changing "God" to "He", they *take out the fact* that *Jesus is God.*
2) Adds the words "*who*" and "*was*" changing the sentence structure and meaning.

20

I Timothy 3:16
(Living Bible)

"It is quite true that the way to live a godly life is *not an easy matter.* But the answer lies in Christ, who came to earth *as a man,* was proved spotless and pure in his Spirit, was served by angels, was preached among the nations, *was accepted by men everywhere* and was received up *again* to his glory *in heaven."*

Notice these changes: (all in *one* verse)

1) It leaves out that *Jesus is God.*

2) "It is *quite* true" is the *opposite* of "without controversy"

3) A "mystery" has nothing to do with not being an "easy matter".

4) The Bible says . . . *"preached* unto the Gentiles" *NOT "accepted* by men everywhere."

    Jesus was NOT "accepted by men everywhere" . . .

Isaiah 53:3 says . . . "He is *despised* and *rejected* of men; a man of sorrows, and acquainted with grief . . ."

5) Completely *leaves out* "seen of angels"

6) *Adds* "in heaven" and "again".

Ladies and gentlemen . . . if you are willing to accept *this* as the "Word of God" just because it has the word "Bible" on it . . . you had just as well be willing to drink bleach out of a cough syrup bottle just because it says "cough syrup" on it!

21

MORE . . . VERSES THAT ATTACK THE DEITY OF CHRIST.

Romans 14:10b "For we shall all stand before the judgement
& 12   seat of *Christ* . . . So then every one of us shall
(King James)   give account of himself to *God.*"

Do you see the logic of it??????

When we stand before the judgement seat of
Christ . . . we are giving account to *God.*

THEREFORE . . . Christ is God!

Romans 14:10b "For we shall all stand before the judgement
& 12   seat of *God* . . . So then each one of us shall
(New American   give account of himself to *God.*"
Standard)

Do you see that? Do you SEE that? Do you see THAT?

Just *one* small word is CHANGED . . . YET . . .

There is *no* proof that Jesus is God in these verses!!!

If a Jehovah's witness ever comes to your door and says,

"Of course we don't believe that Christ is really God. He was the
first being that God created."

If you don't have the REAL Word of God in your home . . . you
may have a hard time proving that Jesus really is God.

Acts 20:28 (King James)	"Take heed, therefore, unto yourselves, and to all the flock, over which the Holy Ghost hath made you overseers, to feed the *church of God,* which he hath purchased with *his own* blood."
Acts 20:28 (Revised Standard Version)*	"Take heed to yourselves and to all the flock, in which the Holy Spirit has made you overseers, to care for the church of God which he obtained with the blood of *his own Son.*"

Did you catch the difference???

In the King James . . . *God's church* was purchased by *God's blood* — THEREFORE . . . <u>*Christ is God.*</u> (it was Christ that shed His blood)

The RSV *separates* Christ from God — PROVING NOTHING! when it changes "*his own* blood" to "the blood of his *own Son*".

SUCH TAMPERING WITH THE WORD OF GOD SHOULD NEVER, EVER BE TOLERATED BY BORN AGAIN BELIEVERS, WHO CLAIM TO LOVE GOD AND HIS WORD!!!

They're pretty tricky, aren't they? Satan is truly a "master of deceit".

*Quoted from Holman edition, copyright 1982. Other editions (e.g. NCC, 1946) may vary.

MORE . . . VERSES ATTACKING
THE DEITY OF CHRIST . . .

John 9:35 (King James)

*"Jesus heard that they had cast him out; and when he had found him, he said unto him, Dost thou believe on the **Son of God?**"*

John 9:35 (New American Standard)

*"Jesus heard that they had put him out; and finding him, He said, "Do you believe in the **Son of Man?**"*

Matthew 4:10

*"Thou shalt **worship** the Lord thy God, and him **only** shalt thou serve,"*

When Jesus *accepted worship,* He admitted that He is God!

Revelation 22:8-9

*"And I John saw these things, and heard them. And when I had heard and seen, **I fell down to worship** before the feet of **the angel** which shewed me these things. Then saith he unto me, **See thou do it not:** for I am thy fellowservant, and of thy brethren the prophets, and of them which keep the sayings of this book: **worship God.**"*

An angel in heaven would not accept worship . . . but Jesus accepted worship because *Jesus is God.*

Acts 10:25-26 *"And as Peter was coming in, Cornelius met him, and fell down at his feet, and **worshipped** him. But Peter took him up, saying, **Stand up; I myself also am a man.**"*

Peter wouldn't accept worship . . . but Jesus accepted worship because He is God!

Matthew 9:18 (King James)

*"While he spake these things unto them, behold, there came a certain ruler, and **worshipped** him, saying, My daughter is even now dead: but come and lay thy hand upon her, and she shall live."*

Matthew 9:18 (New American Standard)

*"While he was saying these things to them, behold, there came a synagogue official, and **bowed down** before him saying, "My daughter has just died; but come and lay Your hand on her, and she will live."*

Matthew 20:20 (King James)

*"Then came to him the mother of Zebedee's children with her sons, **worshipping** him, and desiring a certain thing of him."*

Matthew 20:20 (New American Standard)

*"Then the mother of the sons of Zebedee came to Him with her sons, **bowing down,** and making a request of Him."*

Mark 5:6 (King James)

*"But when he saw Jesus afar off, he ran and **worshipped** him."*

Mark 5:6 (New American Standard)

*"And seeing Jesus from a distance, he ran up and **bowed down** before Him."*

Luke 24:52 (King James)

*"And they **worshipped** him, and returned to Jerusalem with great joy."*

Luke 24:52 (New American Standard)

"And they returned to Jerusalem with great joy." (worship omitted)

"To worship" does NOT mean to "bow down". You can bow down to the Queen of England out of respect, *without* worshipping her.

Of course they want to take out the "worship" from these verses if they don't want to admit that Jesus is God!

MORE . . . verses that attack the Deity of Christ . . .

Hebrews 2:11 (King James)	*"For both he that sanctifieth and they who are sanctified are all of one: for which cause he is not ashamed to call them brethren."*
Hebrews 2:11 (Revised Version)	*"For he who sanctifies and those who are sanctified have all one origin. That is why he is not ashamed to call them brethren."*

1) The RSV *adds* "origin".

2) Christ did *not* have an *origin!!*

> Psalm 90:2 says, "even from *everlasting*
> to *everlasting* thou art God."

3) By saying that Christ had the same origin as man, they are saying that Christ is a *created being*.

THIS VERSE DOESN'T JUST ATTACK THE DEITY OF CHRIST, IT TEACHES FALSE DOCTRINE . . .

THAT CHRIST IS *NOT* GOD!!!

Micah 5:2
(King James)

*"But thou, Bethlehem Ephratah, though thou be little among the thousands of Judah, yet out of thee shall he come forth unto me that is to be ruler in Israel; whose **goings forth** have been from of old, **from everlasting.**"*

Micah 5:2
(Revised
Standard)

*"But you, O Bethlehem, Ephrathah, who are little to be among the clans of Judah, from you shall come forth for me one who is to be ruler in Israel, whose **origin** is from of old, from ancient days."*

1) Christ has *no* "origin"!

2) By saying that Christ was from *"ancient days"* instead of *"from everlasting"* they are saying that Christ had a beginning!

THAT'S BLASPHEMY!!!

I John 2:23 says . . . *"Whosoever **denieth** the Son, the same **hath not the Father.**"*

Mixing the bad with the good!!!!!

In some places they acknowledge the deity of Christ and in other places they deny it.

WHY? WHY? WHY? WHY? WHY?

Satan can't change everything in the Bible . . . He's too smart for that. Have you ever heard of a counterfeit dollar bill that's ORANGE?

REMEMBER . . . GOD *never* contradicts Himself!!!!!!!

27

... Verses attacking the doctrine of
SALVATION BY FAITH ...
... and the ATONEMENT ...

A man was in court one day. He had committed a crime. He was driving 60 mph in a 25 mph zone.

The Judge said, "Sir, your fine is $100.00 or 2 days in jail."

Man: "But Judge, I don't have $100.00, and I don't want to go to jail."

Just then a lawyer stood up and said, "Judge, I would like to pay this man's fine."

The Judge looked at the man and asked, "Will you accept this lawyer's payment of your fine?"

"Oh, yes Sir!" replied the man.

"Then the penalty has been paid. You are free to go."

That's how it happened with us . . .

God looks at man and says . . ."You have committed a crime . . . the penalty is death."

Romans 3:23 says, "For all have sinned . . ."

Romans 6:23 says, "For the wages of sin is death . . ."

Man looks at God and says, "But Sir, I don't want to die, and I have nothing to pay my penalty with."

Just then Jesus stands up and says, "Sir, *I have paid* this man's fine."

Romans 5:8 says,

> *"But God commendeth his love toward us, in that, while we were yet sinners,*
>
> *Christ died for us."*

God looks at man and says, "Will you accept Jesus' payment for your sins?"

"Oh, yes Sir!" you reply.

"Then, the penalty has been paid and you are free to have eternal life!"

I John 1:7 says,

> ". . . And **the blood of Jesus Christ** his Son cleanseth us from all sin."

NOTICE!!!!!

1) Man did not *earn* his salvation.

Titus 3:5 says,

> "**Not by works** of righteousness which we have done, but according to his **mercy he saved us.**"

2) It was the *blood of Christ* that paid for our sins.

. . . Verses attacking the doctrine of salvation by faith . . .

I Peter 2:2 (King James)   "As newborn babes, desire the sincere milk of the word, **that ye may grow thereby.**"

As Christians we grow by using the Word of God.

I Peter 2:2 (Revised Standard)   "Like newborn babes, long for the pure spiritual milk, that by it you may **grow up to salvation.**"

becomes salvation by WORKS!

It is *impossible* to "grow up to salvation". Salvation is a free gift.
We don't "grow up" to it, we don't "work" for it, we don't
"gradually obtain" it.

Acts 16:31 says . . .

*"**Believe** on the Lord Jesus Christ,
and thou shalt be saved . . ."*

NOTICE!!!

1) I Peter 2:2 is changed to teach salvation by works.

2) The words "of the word" have been *omitted,* leaving one to
wonder what the "milk" is.

John 3:36   *"He that **believeth** on the Son hath everlasting
(King James)   life: and he that **believeth not** the Son shall not
                    see life; but the wrath of God abideth on him."*

John 3:36   *"He who **believes** in the Son has eternal life;
(New American   but he who **does not obey** the Son shall not see
Standard)   life, but the wrath of God abides on him."*

Here the verse is changed from God's declaration that is by
believing . . . to salvation is by *obedience.*

Salvation is not obtained by obeying - that's works - Salvation is
obtained by believing!

30

Genesis 12:3   *God promised to Abraham . . . "And I will bless them that bless thee, and curse him that curseth thee: and in thee shall all families of the earth be blessed."*

Jesus fulfilled this promise . . .

Acts 3:25-26 *"Ye are the children of the prophets and of the covenant which God made with our fathers, saying unto Abraham, And in thy seed shall all the kindreds of the earth **be blessed.** Unto you first God, having raised up **his Son Jesus,** sent him to **bless you,** in turning away every one of you from his iniquities.*

We are blessed with salvation
through Jesus!!!!!

Genesis 12:3   *"I will bless those who bless you and him who*
(Revised   *curses you I will curse, and by you all the*
  Standard)   *families of the earth shall **bless themselves."***

INSTEAD of being blessed *through Christ . . .*

they *BLESS THEMSELVES!!!!!*

That's salvation by WORKS!

The *one* major difference between Christianity and the false religions of the world is that they teach that man can save himself (salvation by works of some sort). Here the RSV changes God's Word to say that all the families of the earth shall bless *themselves.* That's the Devil's lie! That one lie has sent more people to Hell than any other lie that he has propounded!

John 6:47
(King James)

"Verily, verily, I say unto you, He that believeth on me hath everlasting life."

John 6:47
(New American
 Standard)

"Truly, truly, I say to you, he who believes has eternal life."

He who believes *what?* The airplane in the sky? The Late, Late Show? The Mickey Mouse Club? The Gong Show? Gilligans Island? The devil? The demons?

They leave out what to believe in . . .

Jesus said . . . "He that believeth ON ME . . ."

John 6:35
(King James)

*"And Jesus said unto them, I am the bread of life: he that cometh to me shall **never hunger;** and he that believeth on me shall **never thirst.**"*

John 6:35
(New American
 Standard)

*"Jesus said to them, "I am the bread of life; he who comes to Me shall **not hunger,** and he who believes in Me shall **never thirst.**"*

WHY??? do they change "never" to "not"? Let me illustrate the difference between never and not.

I can say, "I am *not* hungry, I just ate a big dinner." BUT . . . that doesn't mean that I will never be hungry again. I will probably be hungry for breakfast in the morning.

Jesus said, ". . . he that cometh to me shall NEVER hunger."

Genesis 6:8 (King James)	*"But Noah found **grace** in the eyes of the Lord."*
Genesis 6:8 (New American Standard)	*"But Noah found **favor** in the eyes of the Lord."*

Zech. 9:9 (King James)	*"Rejoice greatly, O daughter of Zion; shout, O daughter of Jerusalem: behold, thy King cometh unto thee: he is just, **and having salvation;** lowly, and riding upon an ass, and upon a colt the foal of an ass."*
Zech. 9:9 (Revised Standard)	*"Rejoice greatly, O daughter of Zion! Shout aloud, O daughter of Jerusalem! Lo, your king comes to you; triumphant and victorious is he, humble and riding on an ass, on a colt the foal of an ass."*

LEAVES OUT - *"and having salvation".*

Col. 1:14 (King James)	*"In whom we have redemption **through his blood,** even the forgiveness of sins."*
Col. 1:14 (New American Standard)	*"in whom we have redemption, the forgiveness of sins."*

LEAVES OUT - *"through his blood".*

The blood of Jesus Christ is the most important part. Of course Satan wants that left out!

I Peter 4:1
(King James)
"Forasmuch then as Christ hath suffered for us in the flesh, arm yourselves likewise with the same mind . . ."

Why did Christ suffer? . . . *for us!*

I Peter 4:1
(New American Standard)
"Therefore since Christ has suffered in the flesh, arm yourselves also with the same purpose."

LEAVES OUT that Christ suffered <u>for us</u>!

. . . verses attacking the resurrection of Christ . . .

Mark 16:9-20
These verses tell about the resurrection of Christ. In the New American Standard Bible they put brackets around all 12 of these verses and say that they were *"probably not"* in the original writings.

That is a *very* misleading statement!
Out of 620 ancient manuscripts of the book of Mark, these 12 verses are found in 618 of them. To say that they were "probably not in the original writings" is *ridiculous!*

Luke 24:6
(King James)
"He is not here, but is risen: *remember how he spake unto you when he was yet in Galilee,"*

Luke 24:6
(Revised Standard)
"Remember how he told you, while he was still in Galilee,"

Did you see that?????? Look again!!!!!!

They LEFT OUT . . . *"He is not here, but is risen."!*

Titus 2:13   *"Looking for that blessed hope, and the*
(King James   ***glorious appearing*** *of the great God and our*
                    Savior Jesus Christ;"

WHAT is the blessed hope that we are looking for???
. . . the *glorious appearing of Christ!!!*

Titus 2:13   *"Looking for the blessed hope and the*
(New American   ***appearing of the glory*** *of our great God and*
Standard)   *Savior, Christ Jesus."*

LOOK! LOOK! LOOK! LOOK! LOOK! LOOK! LOOK!

Here they changed it from the "glorious appearing *of Christ*"
    to . . .
                    the appearing of *"the glory"*.

What kind of "glory" are we supposed to look for? If *that* isn't
CHANGING the Word of God, I don't know what is!!!

It's dangerous to look for a "glory". The anti-Christ will probably
look like a "glory".

I Peter 2:2
(King James)

*"As newborn babes, desire the sincere **milk of the word,** that ye may grow thereby;"*

I Peter 2:2
(Revised
  Standard)

*"Like newborn babes, long for the pure **spiritual milk,** that by it you may grow up to salvation;"*

What is "spiritual milk"? WHO KNOWS?????

The new Christian that reads this verse would *not* know (from the RSV) what he should desire to help him grow.

THE BIBLE SAYS . . . that the *Word of God* is the "milk" that will help him grow.

By taking the Word of God out of this verse, Satan hopes to *starve* newborn Christians.

Luke 4:4
(King James)

*"And Jesus answered him saying, It is written, That man shall not live by bread alone, **but by every word of God."***

Luke 4:4
(New American
  Standard)

"And Jesus answered him, "It is written, Man shall not live on bread alone."

IT LEAVES OUT . . . *"but by every word of God"*!!!!!!
That's the most important part!!

II Timothy 3:16 says . . .   *"All scripture is given by inspiration of God, and is profitable . . ."*

In the footnote of the New American Standard Bible they say, "or, Every scripture inspired by God is also profitable . . ."
This implies that there are Scriptures that are NOT given by inspiration of God.

I Thess. 2:13
(King James)   *"For this cause also thank we God without ceasing, because, when ye received the **word of God** which ye heard of us, ye received it not as the word of men, But as it is in truth, the **word of God** . . ."*

In the New American Standard, they change the "word of God" to the "word of God's *message*"

Instead of the actual word of God, it is just God's *message.*

This is extremely important! If we can't trust the Bible as the actual Word of God, then we don't have any final standard in which we can trust!

VERSES . . . THAT ATTACK THE DOCTRINE OF THE *VIRGIN BIRTH* . . .

Isaiah 7:14
(King James)   *"Therefore the Lord himself shall give you a **sign; Behold a virgin shall conceive** and bear a son, and shall call his name Immanuel."*

Isaiah 7:14
(Revised Standard)   *"Therefore the Lord himself will give you a sign. Behold a **young woman** shall conceive and bear a son and shall call his name Immanuel."*

37

| Isaiah 7:14
(Good News) | *"Well then, the Lord himself will give you a sign: a **young woman who is pregnant*** will have a son and will name him 'Immanuel'."* |

*young women who are pregnant have sons every day - that is not a "sign".

The miracle is that a *virgin* would conceive.

| Matthew 1:22-23
(King James) | *"Now all this was done, **that it might be fulfilled** which was spoken of the Lord by the prophet, saying, Behold a **virgin** shall be with child, and shall bring forth a son, and they shall call his name Emmanuel, which being interpreted is, **God with us**."* |

1) When you deny the virgin birth of Christ . . . you are saying that Christ was an *illegimate child,* since Mary was not married when He was conceived.

2) When you deny the virgin birth of Christ . . . you are saying that Mary was a *fornicator.*

3) When you deny the virgin birth of Christ . . . you are calling God a *liar* in Matthew 1:22-23.

4) When you deny the virgin birth of Christ . . . you are saying that Christ was *not* God. (If he had a physical father, then he was human like you and me.)

5) When you deny the virgin birth of Christ . . . you are saying that Christ was a *sinner,* because he would have had to have a physical father.

> Romans 5:12 says . . . *"Wherefore, as by one man sin entered into the world, and death by sin; and so death passed upon all men, for that all have sinned:"*

38

For MORE *blasphemy* . . . Look in the footnote of the Good News Bible under Isaiah 7:14

"The Hebrew word translated "Young woman" is *not* the particular term for *"virgin"* but refers to any young woman of marriageable age. *The use of "virgin" in Matthew 1:23 reflects a Greek translation of the Old Testament made some 500 years after Isaiah."*

Luke 1:34   *"Then said Mary unto the angel, How shall this*
(King James)   *be, seeing **I know not a man**?"*

Luke 1:34   *"And Mary said to the angel, 'How shall this*
(Revised   *be, since **I have no husband**?"*
Standard)

How dumb do they think we are?

Do women ever have children without having husbands????
   Of course they do!
God was declaring that Mary was a virgin. The RSV tries to cover up this fact.

Luke 2:33   *"And **Joseph** and his mother marvelled at those*
(King James)   *things which were spoken of him."*

Luke 2:33   *"And **His father** and mother were amazed at*
(New American   *the things which were being said about Him."*
Standard)

1) *God* was careful to make it clear that Joseph was *not* Jesus' father.

39

2) When they call Joseph *"His father"* *they deny the virgin birth of Christ.*

3) *In verse 48, Mary calls Joseph his father BUT we are not saying that Mary's* word is perfect, we are saying that *God's* word is perfect!

God NEVER contradicts Himself!!!!!!

After reading this section . . .
of changes, omissions, and misc. errors...
in the modern versions, can you still sit there and say that the modern translations just "update the language" in the Bible?

IF . . . you still try to say that there are *no* doctrinal changes in the modern versions, you might as well go stick your head in the sand . . . like an ostrich.

May I repeat . . .?

*"The words of the Lord are **pure** words: as silver tried in a furnace of earth, purified seven times."*
*"Thou shalt **keep** them, O Lord, thou shalt **preserve** them from this generation **for ever.**"* Psalm 12:6-7

God's Word has *NOT* been preserved in the modern versions, but it *HAS* been preserved in the King James Bible (from the Textus Receptus).

CHAPTER FOUR

THE LIVING BIBLE— COMPARED

The Living Bible is *not* a translation of the Bible, but a paraphrase. That means that Mr. Taylor put the Bible *in his own words.* The problem is that the Living Bible claims to be the word of *God.*

On the back of the student edition of the Living New Testament it says . . .

"Kenneth Taylor began paraphrasing the New Testament for the youth in his own family so they would have God's Word in simple everyday language."

The Living Bible is NOT God's Word! It is man's word! *God's Word* is *perfect* and *infallible,* completely *without error.* The Living Bible is *none* of these.

We do not have the room here to go into all of the things wrong with the Living Bible but will just compare a few verses. If you would like some more information about it you can get the book...

> "The Paraphrased Perversion of the Bible"
> by Gene Nowlin, Ph.D. published by
> "The Bible for Today" Collingswood, N.J.

Mr. Nowlin was a chemist and does a very thorough job of examining this paraphrase in his 297 page book.

ANYWAY . . . Back to the comparison

Rev. 22:18-19 says, *"For I testify unto every man that heareth the*
(King James) *words of the prophecy of this book, If any man*
shall add unto these things, God shall add unto
him the plagues that are written in this book:
And if any man shall take away from the words
of the book of this prophecy, God shall take
away his part out of the book of life, and out of
the holy city, and from the things which are
written in this book."

It's serious business to tamper with the Word of God!

The Living Bible *adds, takes away,* and *changes* God's Word.

John 9:34 *"They **answered** and said unto him, **Thou wast***
(King James) ***altogether** born in sins, and dost thou teach us?*
And they cast him out."

John 9:34 *"**You illegitimate** , **you!**" they **shouted.***
(Living Bible) *"Are you trying to teach us?" And they threw*
him out.

That's perverting
and corrupting
the Word of God!

II Cor. 2:17 says, *"For we are not as many, which **corrupt** the word*
of God.

MORE . . . LIVING BIBLE COMPARED

I Samuel 20:30
(King James)

*"Then Saul's anger was kindled against Jonathan, and he **said** unto him, Thou son of the perverse rebellious woman, . . ."*

I Samuel 20:30
(Living Bible)

*"Saul boiled with rage. '**You son of a**   !' he yelled at him."*

God's Word doesn't use dirty slang! Is this what you want your *children* to read? Don't use the flimsy excuse that it is an "adult" Bible. No one should read dirty language!

I Kings 18:27
(King James)

*"And it came to pass at noon, that Elijah mocked them and said, Cry aloud: for he is a god; either he is **talking,** or he is **pursuing,** or he is in a **journey,** or peradventure he **sleepeth,** and must be awaked."*

I Kings 18:27
(Living Bible)

*"About noontime, Elijah began mocking them. 'You'll have to shout louder than that,' he scoffed, 'to catch the attention of your god! Perhaps he is talking to someone, **or is out sitting on the toilet,** or maybe he is away on a trip, or is asleep and needs to be wakened."*

"pursuing" does NOT mean *"out sitting on the toilet!"*

That is CHANGING God's Word!!!!!!

43

MORE . . . LIVING BIBLE COMPARED

II Kings 21:6b   *". . . he wrought much wickedness **in the sight***
(King James)   *of the Lord, to provoke Him to anger."*

II Kings 21:6b   *". . . So the Lord was very angry, for Manasseh*
(Living Bible)   *was an evil man, **in God's opinion.***"

An opinion can be right or wrong. *God doesn't have an opinion!*
God is always RIGHT!

Psalm 34:20   *"He keepeth all his bones: **not one of them is***
(King James)   **broken.***"

This prophecy concerning Christ was fulfilled in *John 19:36. "For
these things were done, that the **scripture** should be **fulfilled, A
bone of him shall not be broken."***

Psalm 34:20   *"God even protects him **from accidents."***
(Living Bible)

There is no prophecy left in that! That one verse should make you
want to throw your Living "Bible" in the trash!

Zech. 13:6-7   *"And one shall say unto him, What are **these***
(King James)   **wounds in thine hands?** *Then he shall answer,*
                   Those with which I was wounded in the house
                   *of **my friends.** A wake, O sword, against my*
                   shepherd, and against the man that is my
                   *fellow, saith the LORD of hosts: **smite the***
                   shepherd, and the sheep shall be scattered; *and*
                   I will turn mine hand upon the little ones."

This prophecy of Christ concerning the *nail scars* in His hands,
being *wounded* by His *own* people, and His followers (sheep) being
scattered, was fulfilled in *Mark 14:27b.*

Jesus said . . . "for it is written, ***I will smite the shepherd and the
sheep shall be scattered."***

MORE . . . LIVING BIBLE COMPARED

Zech. 13:6-7
(Living Bible)

*"And if someone asks, 'Then what are these scars on your **chest** and your **back**?' he will say, 'I got **into a brawl** at the home of a friend!' Awake O sword against my Shepherd, the man who is my associate and equal, says the Lord of hosts. Strike down the Shepherd and the sheep will scatter, but I will come back and comfort and care for the lambs."*

This is almost unbelievable!
Jesus said in Mark 14:27 that this is a prophecy of Him!

1) They changed, *"wounds in thine hands"* to *"scars on your back"*

2) They changed, *"I was wounded* in the house of my friends" to *"I got into a brawl* at the home of a friend".

Did Christ get into a drunken brawl???

This is *blasphemy* folks!!!!

Then . . . Look at Mr. Taylor's footnote . . .

"Evidently *self-inflicted* cuts, as practiced by *false prophets.*
See I Kings 18:28 . . . That this is *not* a passage referring to Christ is clear from the context. This is a *false prophet* who is lying about his scars."

TIME Magazine
July 24, 1972

"Mysteriously half way through the paraphrase *Taylor lost his voice and still speaks in a hoarse whisper.* A psychiatrist who examined him suggested that the voice failure was Taylor's psychological selfpunishment for *tampering with* what he believed to be *the Word of God."*

John 3:14
(King James)

"And as Moses lifted up the serpent in the wilderness, even so must the Son of man be lifted up."

John 3:14
(Living Bible)

"And as Moses in the wilderness lifted up the **bronze image** *of a serpent* **on a pole,** *even so must I be lifted up* **upon a pole."**

Was Jesus crucified on a pole? NO!!! It was a *cross!* (John 19:25)

NOTICE how much Mr. Taylor *adds* to this verse (8 words). His whole "Bible" is really a commentary, *adding* his opinion of what he thinks the verses *should* say.

Rev. 22:18 says . . . *". . . If any man shall* **add** *unto these things, God shall* **add unto him the plagues** *that are written in this book."*

NOTE: Some later editions of the Living Bible have been revised and some of the exposed verses have been changed. For example in "The Book" (which is what they call the Living Bible now), they changed I Samuel 20:30 to say "you fool." However, this doesn't remedy the hundreds of other places where they "changed the truth of God into a lie."   Romans 1:25

CHAPTER FIVE

OMISSIONS

The verses or phrases that are underlined are OMITTED by the New American Standard Bible either by putting them in brackets and saying, "Brackets in the text are around words *probably not* in the original writings," or by saying in the footnotes that "many mss. do not contain this verse."

Acts 8:36-38a *"And as they went along the road they came to some water; and the eunuch said, "Look! water! What prevents me from being baptized? <u>And Philip said, "If you believe with all your heart, you may." And he answered and said, "I believe that Jesus Christ is the Son of God."</u> And he ordered the chariot to stop . . ." NAS*

Matthew 17:21 *"<u>But this kind does not go out except by prayer and fasting.</u>" NAS*

Matthew 18:11 *"<u>For the Son of Man has come to save that which was lost.</u>" NAS*

Mark 7:16 *"<u>If any man has ears to hear, let him hear.</u>" NAS*

Mark 11:26 *"<u>But if you do not forgive, neither will your Father who is in heaven forgive your transgressions.</u>" NAS*

Mark 15:28	*"And the scripture was fulfilled which says. "And he was numbered with the transgressors."* NAS
Luke 17:36	*"Two men will be in the field; one will be taken and the other will be left."* NAS
Luke 23:17	*"Now he was obliged to release to them at the feast one prisoner."* NAS
Luke 24:11-13a	*"And these things appeared to them as nonsense, and they would not believe them. But Peter arose and ran to the tomb; stooping and looking in, he saw the linen wrappings only; and he went away to his home, marveling at that which had happened. And behold, two of them were going that very day to a village named Emmaus,"* NAS
Luke 24:40	*"And when He had said this, He showed them His hands and His feet,"* NAS
Matthew 23:14	*"Woe to you scribes and Pharisees, hypocrites, because you devour widows' houses, even while for a pretense you make long prayers; therefore you shall receive greater condemnation."* NAS
Mark 9:43b-46	*". . . it is better for you to enter life crippled, than having your two hands, to go into hell, into the unquenchable fire, where their worm does not die and the fire is not quenched. And if your foot causes you to stumble, cut it off; it is better for you to enter life lame, than having your two feet, to be cast into hell, where their worm does not die, and the fire is not quenched."* NAS
Mark 16:9-20	*"Now after He had risen early on the first day of the week, He first appeared to Mary Magdalene, from whom He had cast out seven demons. 10) She went and reported to those who had been with Him, while they were mourning and weeping. 11) And when they heard that He was alive, and had been seen by her, they refused to believe it. 12) And after that, He appeared in a different form to two of them, while*

48

they were walking along on their way to the country. 13) And they went away and reported it to the others, but they did not believe them either. 14) And afterward He appeared to the eleven themselves as they were reclining at the table: and He reproached them for their unbelief and hardness of heart, because they had not believed those who had seen Him after He had risen. 15) And He said to them, "Go into all the world and preach the gospel to all creation, 16) He who has believed and has been baptized shall be saved: but he who has disbelieved shall be condemned. 17) And these signs will accompany those who have believed; in My name they will cast out demons, they will speak with new tongues; 18) they will pick up serpents, and if they drink any deadly poison, it shall not hurt them; they will lay hands on the sick, and they will recover." 19) So then, when the Lord Jesus had spoken to them, He was received up into heaven, and sat down at the right hand of God. 20) And they went out and preached everywhere, while the Lord worked with them, and confirmed the word by the signs that followed." NAS

Matthew
6:9-13

"Pray, then in this way: 'Our Father who art in heaven, Hallowed be Thy name. Thy kingdom come. Thy will be done, On earth as it is in heaven. Give us this day our daily bread. And forgive us our debts, as we also have forgiven our debtors. And do not lead us into temptation but deliver us from evil. For Thine is the kingdom and the power, and the glory, forever, Amen." NAS

Luke
22:19-20

"And when he had taken some bread and given thanks. He broke it and gave it to them, saying, "This is my body which is given for you; do this in remembrance of Me." And in the same way He took the cup after they had eaten saying, "This cup which is poured out for you is the new covenant in My blood." NAS

John
5:3-5

"In these lay a multitude of those who were sick, blind, lame, and withered, waiting for the moving of the waters; for an angel of the Lord went down at certain seasons into the pool, and stirred up the water; whoever then first, after the stirring up of the water, stepped in was made well from whatever disease with which he was afflicted. And a certain man was there, who had been thirty-eight years in his sickness." NAS

Acts
15:34

"But it seemed good to Silas to remain there." NAS

Acts
24:6-8

"And he even tried to desecrate the temple; and then we arrested him. And we wanted to judge him according to our own law. But Lysias the commander came along, and with much violence took him out of our hands, ordering his accusers to come before you. And by examining him yourself concerning all these matters, you will be able to ascertain the things of which we accuse him." NAS

John
7:53-8:11

"And everyone went to his home. 1) But Jesus went to the Mount of Olives, 2) And early in the morning He came again into the temple, and all the people were coming to Him; and He sat down and began to teach them. 3) And the scribes and the Pharisees brought a woman caught in adultery, and having set her in the midst 4) they said to Him, "Teacher, this woman has been caught in adultery, in the very act. 5) Now in the Law Moses commanded us to stone such women; what then do You say? 6) And they were saying this, testing Him, in order that they might have grounds for accusing Him. But Jesus stooped down, and with His finger wrote on the ground. 7) But when they persisted in asking Him, He straightened up, and said to them, "He who is without sin among you, let him be the first to throw a stone at her." 8) And again He stooped down, and wrote on the ground. 9) And when they heard it, they began to go out one by one, beginning with the older ones, and He was left alone, and the woman, where

she had been, in the midst. 10) And straightening up, Jesus said to her, "Woman, where are they? Did no one condemn you?" 11) And she said, "No one Lord." And Jesus said, "Neither do I condemn you; go your way. From now on sin no more." NAS

*"And he knew her not till she had brought forth her **firstborn** son: and he called his name JESUS."*
Matthew 1:25 KJV

"and kept her a virgin until she gave birth to a Son; and he called His name Jesus."
Matthew 1:25 NAS (*Leaves out* "firstborn".)

❋

*"But seek ye first the kingdom **of God**, and his righteousness; and all these things shall be added unto you."*
Matthew 6:33 KJV

"But seek first His kingdom and His righteousness; and all these things shall be added to you." Matthew 6:33 NAS (*Leaves out* "of God".)

❋

*"And, behold, they cried out, saying, What have we to do with thee, **Jesus**, thou Son of God? art thou come hither to torment us before the time?"*
Matthew 8:29 KJV

"And behold, they cried out, saying, 'What do we have to do with You, Son of God? Have You come here to torment us before the time?" Matt. 8:29 NAS (*Leaves out* "Jesus".)

❋

*"For I am not come to call the righteous, but sinners **to repentance"***
Matthew 9:13b KJV

"for I did not come to call the righteous but sinners." Matt. 9:13 NAS (*Leaves out* "repentance".)

❋   ❋

"*A good man out of the good treasure __of the heart__ bringeth forth good things: and an evil man out of the evil treasure bringeth forth evil things.*" Matthew 12:35 KJV

"*The good man out of his good treasure brings forth what is good; and the evil man out of his evil treasure brings forth what is evil.*" Matthew 12:35 NAS (*Leaves out* "of the heart")

"__*Jesus saith unto them,*__ *Have ye understood all these things? They say unto him, Yea,* __*Lord.*__" Matthew 13:51 KJV

"*Have you understood all these things? They said to Him,* "*Yes.*" Matthew 13:51 NAS (*Leaves out* "Jesus saith unto them" and "Lord".)

✼   ✼

"*And in the morning, It will be foul weather today: for the sky is red and lowring.* __*O ye hypocrites,*__ *ye can discern the face of the sky; but can ye not discern the signs of the times?*" Matthew 16:3 KJV

"*And in the morning, 'there will be a storm today, for the sky is red and threatening.' Do you know how to discern the appearance of the sky, but cannot discern the signs of the times?*" Matthew 16:3 NAS (*Leaves out* "O ye hypocrites".)

✼   ✼

"*Then charged he his disciples that they should tell no man that he was* __*Jesus*__ *the Christ.*" Matthew 16:20 KJV

"*Then He warned the disciples that they should tell no one that He was the Christ.*" Matthew 16:20 NAS (*Leaves out* "Jesus".)

✼   ✼

"*And he said unto him, Why callest thou me good? there is none good but one,* __*that is God:*__ *but if thou wilt enter into life, keep the commandments.*" Matthew 19:17 KJV

"*And He said to him,* "*Why are you asking Me about what is good? There is only One who is good; but if you wish to enter into life, keep the commandments.*" Matthew 19:17 NAS (*Leaves out* "God".)

52

*"They say unto him, Because no man hath hired us. He saith unto them, Go ye also into the vineyard; **and whatsoever is right, that shall ye receive.**"* Matthew 20:7 KJV

*"So the last shall be first, and the first last: **for many are called but few chosen.**"* Matthew 20:16 KJV

*"But Jesus answered and said, Ye know not what ye ask, Are ye able to drink of the cup that I shall drink of, **and to be baptized with the baptism that I am baptized with?** They say unto him, We are able."* Matthew 20:22 KJV

*"Watch therefore, for ye know neither the day nor the hour **wherein the Son of man cometh.**"* Matthew 25:13 KJV

*"And they crucified him, and parted his garments, casting lots: **that it might be fulfilled which was spoken by the prophet, They parted my garments among them, and upon my vesture did they cast lots.**"* Matthew 27:35 KJV

They said to him, "Because no one hired us." He said to them, "You too go into the vineyard." Matt. 20:7 NAS (*Leaves out* "and whatsoever is right, that shall ye receive".)

"Thus the last shall be first, and the first last." Matthew 20:16 NAS (*Leaves out* "for many are called but few chosen.")

"But Jesus answered and said, You do not know what you are asking for. Are you able to drink the cup that I am about to drink? They said to Him, "We are able." Matthew 20:22 NAS (*Leaves out* "And to be baptized with the baptism that I am baptized with".)

"Be on the alert then, for you do not know the day nor the hour." Matthew 25:13 NAS (*Leaves out* "wherein the Son of man cometh".)

"And when they had crucified Him, they divided up His garments among themselves, casting lots;" Matt. 27:35 NAS (*Leaves out* "that it might be fulfilled which was spoken by the prophet, They parted my garments among them, and upon my vesture did they cast lots."

"And behold, there was a great earthquake: for the angel of the Lord descended from heaven, and came and rolled back the stone *from the door, and sat upon it.*"
Matthew 28:2 KJV

✸

"*And as they went to tell his disciples, behold, Jesus met them saying, All hail. And they came and held him by the feet, and worshipped him.*"
Matthew 28:9 KJV

✸

"*Now after that John was put in prison, Jesus came into Galilee, preaching the gospel of the kingdom of God.*"
Mark 1:14 KJV

✸

"*When Jesus heard it, he saith unto them, They that are whole have no need of the physician, but they that are sick: I came not to call the righteous but sinners to repentance.*" Mark 2:17 KJV

"*And behold, a severe earthquake had occured, for an angel of the Lord descended from heaven and came and rolled away the stone and sat upon it.*" Matthew 28:2 NAS (*Leaves out* "from the door".)

✸

"*And behold, Jesus met them and greeted them. And they came up and took hold of His feet and worshiped Him.*"
Matthew 28:9 NAS (*Leaves out* "And as they went to tell his disciples".)

✸

"*And after John had been taken into custody, Jesus came into Galilee, preaching the gospel of God.*" Mark 1:14 NAS ("gospel" is not "kingdom".)

✸

"*And hearing this, Jesus said to them 'It is not those who are healthy who need a physician, but those who are sick; I did not come to call the righteous, but sinners.*"
Mark 2:17 NAS (*Leaves out* "to repentance".)

MORE . . . OMISSIONS . . .

You'll have to look them up for yourself but in these verses *words* or *phrases* or even the *whole verse* is missing. Many times they do not even mention it in the footnotes.

Mark 7:16	Luke 24:49	Romans 1:16
Mark 9:24	Luke 24:51	Romans 5:2
Mark 9:42	John 1:14	Romans 9:28
Mark 9:44&46	John 1:18	Romans 11:6
Mark 10:21	John 1:27	Romans 13:9
Mark 11:10	John 3:13	Romans 14:6
Mark 11:26	John 3:15	Romans 14:9
Mark 12:29-30	John 4:42	Romans 14:21
Mark 13:14	John 5:3	Romans 15:29
Mark 15:28	John 5:4	Romans 16:24
Mark 16:9-20	John 6:47	I Cor. 5:7
Luke 1:28	John 7:53-8:11	I Cor. 6:20
Luke 2:33	John 8:16	I Cor. 7:39
Luke 2:43	John 11:41	I Cor. 10:28
Luke 4:4	John 16:16	I Cor. 11:24
Luke 4:8	John 17:12	I Cor. 15:47
Luke 4:41	Acts 2:30	I Cor. 11:29
Luke 7:31	Acts 7:30	I Cor. 16:22
Luke 9:54	Acts 7:37	I Cor. 16:23
Luke 11:29	Acts 8:37	II Cor. 4:6
Luke 22:31	Acts 9:5-6	II Cor. 4:10
Luke 23:17	Acts 10:6	Gal. 3:1
Luke 23:42	Acts 16:31	Gal. 4:7
Luke 24:12	Acts 17:26	Gal. 6:15
Luke 24:40	Acts 20:25	Eph. 3:9

Revelation 22:19 says . . . *"And if any man shall **take away** from the words of the book of this prophecy, **God shall take away** his part out of the book of life, and out of the holy city, and from the things which are written in this book."*

THERE ARE OVER *80* MORE OMISSIONS . . . !!!!!

CHAPTER SIX

WHERE DID OUR KING JAMES BIBLE COME FROM?

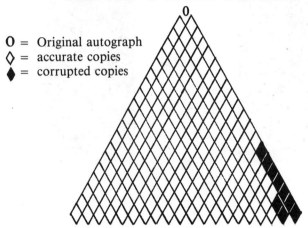

O = Original autograph
◇ = accurate copies
◆ = corrupted copies

ACCURATE COPIES

These manuscripts represent the manuscripts from which the "Textus Receptus" or Received Text, was taken. They are the majority of Greek manuscripts which agree with each other and have been accepted by Bible-believing Christians down through the centuries. It is from these manuscripts that the King James Bible was translated in 1611.

CORRUPTED COPIES

These manuscripts represent the corrupted copies of the Bible, also known as the Alexandrian manuscripts. These manuscripts, many times, do not even agree with each other. The Vaticanus and Siniaticus manuscripts are part of this group. These are the manuscripts on which Westcott and Hort and the modern versions rely so heavily.

There are 5,309 surviving Greek manuscripts that contain all or part of the New Testament.

These manuscripts agree together 95% of the time. The other 5% accounts for the differences between the King James and the modern versions.

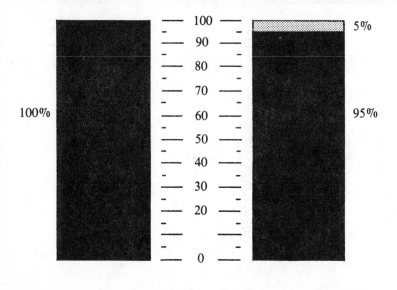

100%

— 100 —
— 90 —
— 80 —
— 70 —
— 60 —
— 50 —
— 40 —
— 30 —
— 20 —
— 0 —

5%

95%

Textus Receptus (King James) does *not* include the Vaticanus & Siniaticus.

Manuscripts from which the modern versions are translated. (Includes the Textus Receptus *plus* the Vaticanus and Siniaticus.)

The modern versions had to use the Textus Receptus, since it contains the majority of surviving Greek manuscripts. The problem is that when the Textus Receptus disagreed with the Vaticanus or the Siniaticus, they preferred these corrupted manuscripts *over* the Textus Receptus. That accounts for the 5% corruption in the modern versions. Even these two manuscripts agree with the Textus Receptus much of the time. When they do not agree, it's because Marcion (120-160 AD) or Origin (184-254 AD) or whoever, CORRUPTED them.

NOW . . . the fact has been established that the modern versions are DIFFERENT than the King James Bible
BUT . . .

we still need to answer the question of . . .

WHY . . . are they different?

There are at least 5,309 surviving Greek manuscripts which contain all or part of the New Testament. PLUS . . . there are translations into different languages which date back to within 100 years of the disciples. For example the Peshitta is a Syrian translation from the 2nd century.

These manuscripts AGREE with each other about 95% of the time.

The problem is . . .
"How does one determine what is right in the 5% of the places where the manuscripts do not agree?"

Argument I
(Modern versions) "The Bible is just like any other book. It is **not** liable to Satanic attack. In order to find out what the original copy probably said, you just find the oldest copies available and use them. We don't have the exact word of God now anyway, so a few disagreements will not matter."

Argument II
(King James) "The Bible is **not** 'just like any other book'. Satan hates it because it is the Word of God. Satan has been trying to destroy it ever since the Garden of Eden. However . . . God has preserved His Word for us. **He preserved the Old Testament through the Levites as priests and He has preserved the New Testament through the body of believers through the witness of the Holy Spirit."**

The vast majority of Greek manuscripts agree together. They have been passed down through the centuries by true Bible-believing Christians. In 1516 Erasmus compiled, edited, and printed the Greek "Textus Receptus" (received text). This is the text that the

Protestants of the reformation **knew** to be the Word of God (inerrant and infallible). The King James Bible was translated from the "Textus Receptus".

Argument I
(Modern versions) The oldest surviving manuscripts must be the most reliable. Therefore . . . when determining what manuscripts to depend on, the Vaticanus (350 AD) and the Siniaticus (about 350 AD) should be accepted as correct (even if 998 other manuscripts disagree with them).

Argument II
(King James) "The oldest manuscripts (the Vaticanus and Siniaticus) are NOT reliable at all!

For one thing . . . the Vaticanus and Siniaticus **disagree** with **each other** over 3,000 times in the gospels alone!

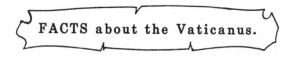

FACTS about the Vaticanus.

It was written on fine vellum (tanned animal skins) and remains in excellent condition. It was found in the Vatican Library in 1481 AD. In spite of being in excellent condition, it omits **Genesis** 1:1-Gen. 46:28, **Psalms** 106-138, **Matt.** 16:2-3, the **Pauline Pastoral Epistles, Hebrews** 9:14-13:25, and all of **Revelation.** These parts were probably left out on purpose.

Besides all that — in the gospels alone it leaves out 237 words, 452 clauses and 748 whole sentences, which hundreds of later copies agree together as having the same words in the same places, the same clauses in the same places and the same sentences in the same places.

The Vaticanus was available to the translators of the King James Bible, but they didn't use it because they knew it is **unreliable.** The Vaticanus also contains the Apocrypha.

The Siniaticus is a manuscript that was found in 1844 in a trash pile in St. Catherine's Monestary near Mt. Sinai, by a man named Mr. Tischendorf. It contains nearly all of the New Testament plus it adds the "Shepherd of Hermes" and the "Epistle of Barnabas" to the New Testament.

The Siniaticus is **extremely** unreliable, proven by examining the manuscript itself. John Burgon spent years examining every available manuscript of the New Testament. He writes about the Siniaticus . . .

"On many occasions 10, 20, 30, 40 words are dropped through very carelessness. Letters, words or even whole sentences are frequently written twice over, or begun and immediately canceled; while that gross blunder, whereby a clause is omitted because it happens to end in the same words as the clause proceeding, occurs no less than 115 times in the New Testament."

THAT'S NOT ALL!!!

On nearly every page of the manuscript there are corrections and revisions, done by 10 different people. Some of these corrections were made about the same time that it was copied, but most of them were made in the 6th or 7th century.

Phillip Mauro was a brilliant lawyer who was admitted to the bar of the Supreme Court in April 1892. He wrote a book called "Which Version" in the early 1900's. He writes concerning the Siniaticus...

"From these facts, therefore, we deduce: first that the **impurity** of the Codex Sinaiticus, in every part of it, was fully recognized by those who were best acquainted with it, and that from the very beginning until the time when it was **finally cast aside** as **worthless** for any practical purpose."

THE VATICANUS AND SINIATICUS MANUSCRIPTS ARE THE OLDEST, BUT . . .

THEY ARE *NOT* THE BEST MANUSCRIPTS!!!!!!!!

That's where the modern translators went wrong!!! They foolishly accepted the Vaticanus and Siniaticus simply because they were **old.**

They did not attempt to find out **WHY** they were so vastly different from the Greek text that real Christians have **known** to be the infallible Word of God.

NOTE: When the modern versions say in the footnotes,

"Some of the oldest mss. do not contain vv. 9-20"

or

"This verse not found in the most ancient authorities" . . .

. . . THEY ARE TAKING THEIR INFORMATION FROM THE *CORRUPT* AND *UNRELIABLE* VATICANUS AND SINIATICUS MANUSCRIPTS!!

Don't fall for the "oldest are the best" line! The oldest are **not** the best!

FOR EXAMPLE: The Vaticanus and Siniaticus both **leave out** the last 12 verses of Mark, concerning the resurrection of Christ.

BUT . . .

. . . there is **not one other** manuscript, either uncial or cursive that leave out this passage. There are 18 other uncial (capital letter) manuscripts that have the passage in and at least 600 cursives (small letter) manuscripts that all CONTAIN these verses.

> **THE EVIDENCE IS AT LEAST 618 TO 2!**

The EVIDENCE is at least 618 to 2
<u>against</u> the Vaticanus and Siniaticus

YET . . .

Look in your modern version . . . the New American Standard Bible puts all these verses (Mark 16:9-20) in brackets, saying that these verses PROBABLY were not in the original writings. The other versions use brackets or footnotes.

THAT'S RIDICULOUS!!!

"Professing themselves to be wise, they became fools . . . Who changed the truth of God into a lie . . ." Romans 1:22&25a

In a court of law . . . if you had 618 witnesses that saw something happen, and you had witnesses that said they did not see it happen . . . Would you accept the testimony of the 618 or the testimony of the 2?

You see, it is foolish for any translator to accept a manuscript simply because of age, without checking to find out where it came from and if it was reliable or not.

Galatians 1:6 says . . . *"I marvel that ye are so soon removed from him that called you into the grace of Christ unto another gospel."*

Please don't get angry . . . We are not saying all this with a spirit of bitterness, but just want you to know the **truth.**

Jesus said, *"And ye shall know the **truth**, and the truth shall make you free."* John 8:32

WHY . . . do the modern version question the **virgin birth** of Christ, attack the doctrine of the **diety** of Christ, the **infallibility** of the Bible, the doctrine of **salvation** by faith and the **Trinity?**

One of the most famous of the early "Bible corrupters" was a man named **Origen.** He lived from 184-254 AD, in Alexandria Egypt. He had a school there. Origen did not believe that the Bible was the infallible Word of God and he felt free to change it if he didn't like what it said. He wrote commentaries on most of the books of the Bible. It was through his influence that the Vaticanus and Siniaticus manuscripts were probably corrupted.

Origen was NOT a Christian!

The New Standard Encyclopedia, vol. 9 pg. 0-155

"One of the most notable of Origen's ideas was his Logos Doctrine. This idea had been expressed in John 1:1-5 and in other Christian writings but Origen gave it the fullest treatment. In **Greek philosophy** Logos was the name of the divine principle of creation and rational world order. Origen applied this principle to Christ's person and work. **Subordinating** the Son to the Father, he treated Christ as the Logos **(created by God)** who brings reason to the world. In this treatment he **neglected the figure of Jesus Christ as a man who lived and taught on earth.** This doctrine provided the foundation for the fourth century Arian Doctrine."

Origen believed like the Jehovah's Witnesses do today - that Jesus is **not** God, but is a created being.

Origen did not even believe that Jesus lived physically on earth! There were many contradictions in Origen's writings. This explains the contradiction in the corrupted manuscripts. Sometimes he would say he accepted the deity of Christ and then he would turn around and deny it.

By the way — Origen did not get his heretical ideas from John 1:1-5. He "corrupted" John 1:1 to say, "the word was **a** god," like the Jehovah's Witnesses do today.

You can thank Origen for the corruption of the Vaticanus and Siniaticus, and you can thank the Vaticanus and Siniaticus for the corruption of the modern versions.

THE BIBLE SAYS:

*"Preach the word; be instant in season, out of season; reprove, rebuke, **exhort** with all longsuffering and doctrine.*

*For the time will come when they **will not** endure sound doctrine; but after their own lusts shall heap to themselves teachers, having **itching ears**;*

*And they shall **turn away** their ears from the **truth**, and shall be **turned unto fables**."* II Timothy 4:2-4

(Now . . . don't get mad at us . . . God's the One who wrote it, we just quote it.)

Don't get depressed . . . God has not been defeated! We still DO have His Word . . . *"But **thanks** be to God which giveth us the **victory** through our Lord Jesus Christ."*

*"Therefore my beloved brethren, be ye steadfast, unmoveable, always abounding in the work of the Lord, forasmuch as ye know that **your labour is not in vain** in the Lord."* I Cor. 15:57-58

"IF ALL THAT YOU SAY IS TRUE . . . THEN WHY DOESN'T MY PREACHER BELIEVE IT???????

No one can speak for your preacher but himself . . . but here are some possible answers.

1) He may not have studied it for himself yet. Maybe no one has ever told him the truth. I was talking to a preacher about this one day and he said, "I've never even heard about that before."

2) It is possible that he was taught in college or seminary that . . .

   a) . . . there are not any important differences between the King James Bible and the modern versions. (we've proved that false)

   b) Perhaps he was told, ". . . when you have a church you will preach out of the King James Bible because so many of the lay people believe that it is the perfect Word of God. But WE know that we don't actually have the perfect Word of God **today.** It was only perfect when it was written by Peter, Paul, Matthew and John etc. . . but alas! the original copies have long been lost."
   (He must not realize that he is actually **lying** to his people if he tells them, "the Word of God is perfect" when he really believes that the Bible has errors in it.)

3) Maybe he realizes that some "translations" are bad but he may be afraid to speak out against them . . . because it is not always popular to tell the truth.

4) He may not want to make waves and thinks that it is not an important enough issue to bring up.

   (Since when is the Word of God not "important"?)

YES! Some translators don't believe the Word of God anyway so they don't mind changing the Bible to fit their personal views.

OTHERS . . . have accepted the teaching of the so-called "scholars" and haven't checked it out for themselves.

"Can you prove that some translators do not believe the Bible?"

"YES"

Quotes from Mr. Hort's autobiography . . .

"**Evangelicals** seem to me **perverted** rather than untrue . . ."

"But the book that has most engaged me is **Darwin** . . . My feeling is strong that the theory is **unanswerable**."

"I have been persuaded for many years that **Mary-worship** and Jesus-worship have very much in common . . ."

"But you know that I am a staunch **sacerdotalist**."
(belief in the sacraments)

"I am inclined to think that such a state as Eden (I mean the popular notion) never existed."

"The popular **doctrine of substitution is an immoral** and material **counterfeit**."

Quotes from Mr. Westcott's autobiography . . .

"I wish I could see to what forgotten truth Mariolatry bears witness."

"No one now, I suppose, holds that the first three chapters of Genesis, for example, gives a literal history."

WHO WERE WESTCOTT AND HORT?????

They were two professors at Cambridge University who lived in the late 1800's. They did not like the King James Bible so they wrote their own revised Greek Text. When he was only 23 Mr. Westcott said, ". . . the **vile** Textus Receptus . . ."

These two men are very important in the history of the modern versions because the text that they wrote is the one that became the basis for the **Revised Standard,** and **many other** modern translations of the Bible.

Now . . . Remember . . . We are **not** saying that ALL translators of modern versions do not believe the Bible. But you need to know that at least some of them were (or are) unbelievers.

What in the world is a Bible-believing Protestant doing, using a Bible that Mr. Hort helped to produce? Just one more quote . . .

"The Romish view seems to me nearer, and more likely to lead to the truth than the Evangelical . . . We dare not forsake the sacraments or God will forsake us."

Mr. Hort wrote this to Mr. John Ellerton, July 6, 1848.

Would **you** trust a translation . . . where the DIRECTOR believed THIS???

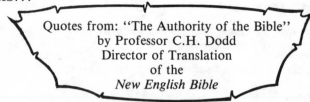

Quotes from: "The Authority of the Bible"
by Professor C.H. Dodd
Director of Translation
of the
New English Bible

"The old dogmatic view of the Bible therefore, is not only open to attack from the standpoint of science and historical criticism, but **if taken seriously** it **becomes a danger** to religion and public morals." page 14 (The Bible is a danger?)

"God is the author, **not** of the Bible **but** of the life in which the authors of the Bible partake, and of which they tell in such **imperfect human words** as they could command." page 17

(God did **not** write the Bible?)

"The most downright claims to infallibility are made by the apocalyptist, as for example in the New Testament Revelation (see 22:6, 16, 18-19) a book which some of the wisest thinkers of the early Church wished to exclude from the canon, and which as a whole, is **sub-Christian** in tone and outlook." page 15
(Revelation is "sub-Christian"?)

"God so loved the world that He gave His only begotten Son - The expression evidently **Anthropomorphic**. It is a **mythological** way of saying that in Christ God gives of His own Being . . ." (John 3:16 is a myth?)

"**Moses has left us no writings,** and we know little of him with certainty." page 27 (Exodus 24:4 says, "*And Moses wrote all the words of the LORD.*")

"For indeed the bare idea of vicarious expiation (substitutionary atonement) is **not wholly rational** . . ." page 215 (I Peter 3:18 says, "*For Christ also hath once suffered for sins . . .*")

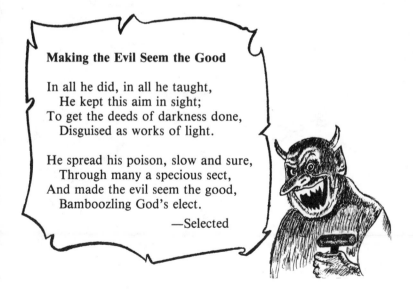

Making the Evil Seem the Good

In all he did, in all he taught,
    He kept this aim in sight;
To get the deeds of darkness done,
    Disguised as works of light.

He spread his poison, slow and sure,
    Through many a specious sect,
And made the evil seem the good,
    Bamboozling God's elect.

—Selected

CHAPTER SEVEN

LOGIC

FACT: The King James Bible is different from the modern translations.

FACT: The Revised Greek Text (from which modern translations are taken) is different from the Textus Receptus (from which the King James Bible is taken) in **5,337 places.**

FACT: The modern translators admit that they are different.

FACT: The modern translations downgrade or deny the **Deity** of Christ, the **virgin birth** of Christ, the **blood atonement** of Christ, the **resurrection** of Christ and the **reliability** of the Word of God.

QUESTION: "Is there such a thing as the Word of God?"

YES ☐   NO ☐

THE BIBLE SAYS:

"For this cause also thank we God without ceasing, because, when ye received the word of God which ye heard of us, ye received it not as the word of men, but as it is in truth, the word of God . . ."
I Thess. 2:13

NOTICE: Paul said that the words that he was writing were the Word of God!

YES, there is such a thing as the Word of God!

QUESTION: "Is the Word of God perfect and without error?
YES ☐ NO ☐

THE BIBLE SAYS:

*"The law of the LORD IS **perfect**, converting the soul: the testimony of the LORD IS **sure**, making wise the simple. The statutes of the LORD are **right**, rejoicing the heart: the commandment of the LORD is **pure**, enlightening the eyes."*
Psalm 19:7&8

YES, the Word of God is perfect and without error!

QUESTION: Is it possible for God to contradict Himself?
YES ☐ NO ☐

THE BIBLE SAYS:

*"In hope of eternal life, which God, **that cannot lie,** promised before the world began." Titus 1:2*

NO, God cannot contradict Himself. He cannot lie!

Do we have the perfect Word of God **TODAY?**

THAT'S THE BIG QUESTION!

FACT: The King James Bible and the new translations are *DIFFERENT*.

THEREFORE . . . . .
We have one of three choices.

EITHER . . . . .

1. The King James Version (translated from the Textus Receptus) is the Word of God.

2. The modern translations are the Word of God.

3. NEITHER is the **perfect** Word of God. We do not have the perfect Word of God today. THEY ARE **BOTH** WRONG.

CONCLUSION

WHICH DO YOU CHOOSE???????

1) If . . . the King James is right . . .

    THEN . . . the modern translations are WRONG . . .

2) IF . . . the modern translations are RIGHT . . .

    Then . . . the King James is WRONG . . .

3) If . . . they are BOTH wrong . . .

    THEN . . . God is a liar . . . God promised that we would have His Word **forever.** If we don't have it today, then He lied.

THE BIBLE SAYS:
"The grass withereth, the flower fadeth: but the word of our God shall stand forever." Isaiah 40:8

*"Heaven and earth shall pass away: but my words **shall not** pass away."*
Luke 21:33

Two contradicting statements **can not both** be right!

GOD CANNOT CONTRADICT HIMSELF!!!

TO TELL THE TRUTH!

BROTHERS AND SISTERS IN CHRIST!!!!
THERE CAN ONLY BE **ONE ABSOLUTELY TRUE,**
INERRANT (WITHOUT ERROR), INFALLIBLE (WITHOUT
FAILING), WORD OF GOD.

THE BIBLE SAYS:

*"For the **prophecy** came not in old time by the will of man: but holy men of God spake as they were moved by the Holy Ghost."*
II Peter 1:21

*"**All scripture** is given by inspiration of God, and is profitable for doctrine, for reproof, for correction, for instruction in righteousness:"* II Timothy 3:16

*"Add thou not unto **His words,** lest he reprove thee and thou be found a liar."* Proverbs 30:6

*"For we are not as many, which corrupt the **word of God:** . . ."*
II Corinthians 2:17

*"**Forever,** O LORD, thy word **is settled** in heaven."* Psalm 119:89

*"I will worship toward thy holy temple . . . for thou hast magnified thy word **above all thy name."*** Psalm 138:2

How do we **know** that the Bible is authentic?

It's like the law of gravity - You can't see it, but you see the results - so you believe it.

*"**The words of the LORD** are pure words: as silver tried in a furnace of earth, purified seven times. Thou shalt keep them, O LORD, thou shalt **preserve** them from this generation **for ever.** "*
Psalm 12:6-7

A Case for the Absolute Reliability of the Bible.

Can I as a Christian, stand up
and hold a Bible in my hand
and say . . .

"This book is the Word of God. It is true! I can trust it. It's perfect, there are no mistakes in it. Thank God for His Word!"

or do I have to say . . .

"This book was perfect when it was written, but that was over 1800 years ago and alas! the original copies are long lost. So . . . even though there are errors, I **hope** that I can trust it and I hope maybe I'll get to heaven some day."

There are three views concerning the reliability of the Bible.

   I. The Bible is completely reliable.
  II. The Bible is somewhat reliable.
 III. The Bible is about as reliable as a book of fairy tales.

Let's examine these views . . .

View I. (The Bible is *completely* reliable)

A. The Bible is the Word of God.
   "For this cause also thank we God without ceasing, because, when ye received the word of God which ye heard of us, ye received it not as the word of men, but as it is in truth, the word of God." I Thess. 2:13
B. The Word of God is perfect - without error.
   "Every word of God is pure . . ." Proverbs 30:5
   "Sanctify them through thy truth: thy word is truth." John 17:17
C. God has miraculously **preserved** His Word for us, so that we have it **today,** without error.
   "But the word of the Lord endureth forever . . ." I Peter 1:25
   For verily I say unto you, Till heaven and earth pass, one jot or one tittle shall in no wise pass from the law, till all be fulfilled." Matt. 5:18

75

View II. (The Bible is *somewhat* reliable)

A. The Bible **was** the Word of God, when it was **originally** written.

The "Foreword" in the New American Standard Bible says:

> "The New American Standard Bible has been produced with the conviction that the words of scripture **as originally penned** in the Hebrew and Greek **were** inspired by God."

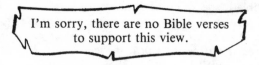

I'm sorry, we do not have any Bible verses to support this view.

B. On page ix, the Revised Standard version says . . .

> "Cn indicates a **correction** made where the text has suffered in transmission and the versions provide **no satisfactory** restoration but the Committee agrees with the judgement of competent scholars as to the most **probable** reconstruction of the original text."

The Preface says . . .

> "Yet **the King James Version has grave defects.**"
> and
> "The King James Version of the New Testament was based upon a Greek text that was **marred by mistakes.**"

I'm sorry, there are no Bible verses to support this view.

View III. The Bible is about as reliable as a book of fairy tales.

A. Professor C.H. Dodd was the director of translation for the New English Bible. He wrote a book called, "The Authority of the Bible." He said . . .

> "God so loved the world that He gave His only begotten Son - the expression is evidently Anthropomorphic. It is a **mythological** way of saying that in Christ God gives of His own Being the utmost that it is possible for humanity to receive of God."

B. Bishop Brooke Westcott and Dr. Fenton Hort were the leaders of the revision committee of 1881 which came up with the Revised Version of the Bible. Most modern versions are taken from the Revised Greek text which they wrote. They did not believe that the Bible was reliable.

These are quotes from their autobiographies . . .

Mr. Hort - "Evangelicals seem to me **perverted** rather than untrue. There are, I fear, **still more serious differences** between us on the subject of authority, and **especially the authority of the Bible.**"

Mr. Westcott in a letter to the Archbishop of Canterbury
March 4, 1890

"No one now, I suppose, holds that the first three chapters of Genesis, for example, give a literal history."

(Galatians 1:8-9 says . . . *"But though we, or an angel from heaven preach any other gospel unto you than that which we have preached unto you, **let him be accursed.** As we said before, so say I now again, If any man preach any other gospel unto you than that ye have received, **let him be accursed.**")*

CHAPTER EIGHT

COPYRIGHTS ©

Look in the front of your Bible. Has it been copyrighted?

Revised Standard Version - copyright 1952 by the National Council of Churches (this is the Council of Churches that is considering admitting the ''Metropolitan Churches'' for Gays.)

New American Standard - copyright 1977 by the Lockman Foundation.

Living Bible - copyright 1971 by Tyndale House Publishers.

Good News Bible - copyright 1976 by the American Bible Society.

Phillips N.T. - copyright by J.B. Phillips (1972)

New International Bible - copyright 1973 by the New York Bible Society.

New Scofield - only the notes are copyrighted, 1967 by the Oxford University Press.

IS THE KING JAMES BIBLE COPYRIGHTED???????
NO!!!!!
WHY????? You cannot copyright **God's** Word!!!!!

You can only copyright **man's** words!!!!!

The copyright makes it ILLEGAL to copy the modern "scripture" versions without the publishers permission.

They may try to "bind" the Word of God . . .
But . . . the Bible says, (Paul speaking)

"Wherein I suffer trouble, as an evil doer, even unto bonds; but the Word of God is not bound." II Timothy 2:9

By taking out a copyright on a so-called "Bible" . . . the copyright owner **admits** that this is **not** "God's Word" BUT **"their own words"** (see the definition of a "copyright" below)

Definition of a "copyright"
New Standard Encyclopedia vol. 3, page 565 . . .

"The legal protection given to **authors** and artists to prevent reproduction of **their** work without their consent. The owner of a copyright has the **exclusive** right to print, reprint, publish, copy and **sell** the material covered by the copyright."

NOTE: Thomas Nelson Co. has a copyright notice in the front of the old King James Bibles that they print. It makes it *appear* that they have the copyright to the King James Bible.

HOWEVER . . . If you call the Thomas Nelson Company, they will tell you that they do not have a copyright on the King James *text* (the Bible itself). What they have copyrighted are the notes and the layout.

CHAPTER NINE

DANGER

Romans 1:22-23
*"Professing themselves to be wise, they became fools,
And changed the glory of the uncorruptible God into an image
made like to corruptible man, and to birds, and fourfooted beasts,
and creeping things."*

Ezekiel 13:3
*"Thus saith the Lord God; Woe unto the
foolish prophets, that follow their own
spirit, and have seen nothing!"*

Isaiah 5:20
*"Woe unto them that call evil good, and good evil; that put
darkness for light and light for darkness; that put bitter for sweet,
and sweet for bitter!"*

Ezekiel 34:2
*". . . Thus saith the Lord God unto the
shepherds; Woe be to the shepherds of
Israel that do feed themselves! should not
the shepherds feed the flocks?"*

Jeremiah 23:1
*"Woe be unto the pastors that destroy
and scatter the sheep of my pasture! saith
the Lord."*

Ezekiel 5:6,8
*"And she hath changed my judgments into wickedness
more than the nations . . . Therefore thus saith the Lord*

God; Behold, I, even I, am against thee, and will execute judgments in the midst of thee in the sight of the nations.''

Revelation 22:18-19
"For I testify unto every man that heareth the words of the prophecy of this book, If any man shall **add** unto these things, God shall add unto him the plagues that are written in this book:
And if any man shall **take away** from the words of the book of this prophecy, God shall take away his part out of the book of life, and out of the holy city, and from the things which are written in this book.''

DON'T FALL INTO THE DEVIL'S TRAP!

"For among my people are found wicked men: they lay wait, as he that setteth snares: they set a trap, they catch men. As a cage is full of birds, so are their houses full of deceit. . ."
Jeremiah 5:26-27

"Be sober, be **vigilant**, because your adversary the devil, **as a roaring lion**, walketh about, **seeking whom he may devour**.''
I Peter 5:8

82

CHAPTER TEN

IT TAKES GUTS TO STAND

"Stand therefore, having your loins girt about with truth. . ." Eph. 6:14

"Sanctify them through thy truth: thy word is truth." John 17:17

Jesus said, *"I am the way, the truth, and the life: no man cometh unto the Father, but by me."* John 14:6

But, WHY is it so important what Bible I use?

1) It's important for your own spiritual good.

THE BIBLE SAYS:

"As newborn babes, desire the sincere milk of the word, that ye may grow thereby:" I Peter 2:2

Why should you drink the **spoiled, diluted, phony,** so-called "milk" of the modern versions?

2) It's **wrong** (sinful) for us to teach our children that we have no absolutely true word of God today. (60 contradicting "Bibles" aren't ALL the truth!)
THE BIBLE SAYS:

*"And these words, which I command thee this day, shall be in thine heart: And thou shalt **teach** them **diligently** unto thy children, and shalt talk of them **when** thou sittest in thine house, and **when** thou walkest by the way, and **when** thou liest down, and **when** thou risest up."* Deut. 6:6-7

3) It's important because we do not want to make the devil happy.

Satan is trying to **disarm** the Christian today. Are you going to let him take away **your** sword without putting up a fight?

If Satan is the one behind the new Bibles . . . What could be his purpose?

1) In Russia and China, Bibles are **outlawed** and are not available to the common person.
   . . . In America . . . the Bible **will not have to be** outlawed. Christians are accepting "counterfeit" Bibles. The **real** Word of God is becoming less and less used.

2) The new versions are one more push down the road to a **one world church.** The New International Version advertises . . . "the work is international . . . also thoroughly **transdenominational.** This new translation will be accepted widely."

Maybe the new versions take away the deity of Christ in some places, but they acknowledge His deity in other places . . .

1) That's Satan's old "contradiction trick." Sometimes he puts it in, sometimes he changes it and sometimes he takes it out.

MIXING THE BAD WITH THE GOOD.
Don't fall for it!

2) God has a purpose for EVERY word in the Bible!

The Bible contains . . . 3,568,489 **letters**
        810,697 **words**
        31,175 **verses**
       1,189 **chapters**

Jesus said . . . "And it is easier for heaven and earth to pass, than **one tittle** *of the law to fail."* Luke 16:17

Don't you know that just about EVERYONE endorses the modern versions?

Just because **"everyone does it"** does not make it right!!!!!

THE BIBLE SAYS:

*"Enter ye in at the strait gate: for **wide** is the gate, and broad is the way, that **leadeth to destruction,** and **many** there be which go in thereat: Because strait is the gate, and **narrow** is the way, which leadeth **unto life,** and **few** there be that find it."* Matthew 7:13-14

"The modern versions just use more "up to date" language . . . There are not any **doctrinal** differences . . . are there?"

When the deity of Christ is attacked in I Timothy 3:16, Romans 14:10&12, Acts 10:28, and John 9:35 . . .

THAT'S DOCTRINE!

When the virgin birth is attacked in Isaiah 7:14, and Luke 1:34 . . .

THAT'S DOCTRINE!

When they take out that Jesus was worshipped in Luke 24:52, Matthew 20:20, Matthew 9:18, and Mark 5:6 . . .

THAT'S DOCTRINE!

When they teach salvation by works in John 3:36 and I Peter 2:2 (RSV) . . .

THAT'S DOCTRINE!

When the "blood" of Christ is taken out of the "Good News Bible" (really the "Bad News Bible") in Matt. 27:4, Matt. 27:24, Matt. 27:25, Acts 5:28, Acts 20:28, Romans 3:25, Romans 5:9, Ephesians 1:7, Eph. 2:13, Col. 1:14, Col. 1:20, Heb. 10:19, I Peter 1:9, Rev. 1:5, and Rev. 5:9 . . .

THAT'S DOCTRINE!

When the atonement is taken out of Col. 1:14 and I Peter 4:1 (for us) . . .

THAT'S DOCTRINE!

"If I don't understand part of the Bible, I don't use it anyway . . . so why should I complain if some translations leave out a few hundred words of phrases????"

THE BIBLE SAYS:

> *"And if any man shall **take away** from the words of the book of this prophecy,   God shall **take away** his part out of the book of life . . ."* Rev. 22:19

"But if I take a stand . . . my preacher friends will call me radical and my friends will say that I'm 'narrow-minded' ."

THE BIBLE SAYS:

> *"**For I am not ashamed** of the gospel of Christ: for it is the power of God unto salvation to every one that believeth . . ."* Romans 1:16

"but . . . I just read the modern versions because they help me understand the Bible better."

Would you drink a glass of water each day, that has "only" one tablespoon of arsenic in it?

It would be 95% pure water and only 5% arsenic.

Of course you wouldn't!
So . . . Why should you read a "Bible" every day that is 5% corrupt?
BE CONSISTENT!!!!!

"What should I do with my modern versions of the Bible?"

Throw them away!

Would you keep a package of spoiled hamburger meat in the refrigerator for the next 6 months, just because you paid $6.95 for it?

Of course not! So why should you keep corrupt Bibles around the house?

"But I can't afford a new King James Bible . . ."

Buy $10.00 less groceries next month and buy a Bible.

Jesus said, *"It is written, Man shall **not live by bread alone,** but by **every** word that proceedeth out of the mouth of God."* Matthew 4:4

NOTICE!!!! It says **"every"** word. Don't use a Bible that leaves out hundreds of words, phrases, and verses!

"It's not right for you to 'judge' these other Bibles and say that they are wrong."

I John 4:1 says, *"Beloved, believe **not every spirit,** but __try__ the spirits whether they are of God: because **many** false prophets are gone out into the world."*

"I know that the KJV is the right Bible, but I don't want to **confuse** my congregation . . . It's such a complicated subject."

You don't have any excuse now . . . just give them a copy of this booklet . . . It's simple enough.

Your people are **already** confused by 60 different Bibles that say different things. It's YOUR job to clear up the confusion!

"I preach out of the King James, although I study out of the modern versions and believe that they are probably better."

That's even worse . . . that's being a hypocrite.

II Timothy 2:15 says, *"Study to shew thyself approved unto God, a workman that needeth not to be ashamed, rightly dividing the Word of truth."*

Last eve I paused beside a blacksmith's door
And heard the anvil ring the vesper chime;
Then looking in, I saw upon the floor
Old hammers worn with beating years of time.

"How many anvils have you had?" said I,
"To wear and batter all these hammers so?"
"Just one," said he, and then with twinkling eyes,
"The anvil wears the hammers out you know."

And so, I thought, "The anvil of God's Word
For ages skeptic blows have beat upon;
Yet, though the noise of falling blows was heard,
The Anvil is unharmed, the hammers GONE."

CHAPTER ELEVEN

IF YOU ARE A PREACHER . . .

. . . AND you haven't taken the time to study the modern versions yet and haven't found out for yourself what is the truth . . .

. . . THEN, start studying!!!!! Get the books and check it out!!!

IT'S IMPORTANT!!!

THE SPIRITUAL LIVES OF YOUR PEOPLE DEPEND ON IT . . . IT'S **YOUR** RESPONSIBILITY!!!!!

IF YOU ARE A PREACHER . . .

. . . and you don't believe that we have the perfect, infallible Word of God today . . .

THEN . . . What in the world are you doing in the ministry???

YOU HAVE **NO** GOOD NEWS TO TELL . . .

IF God was lying when He said,

*"The grass withereth, the flower fadeth: but the word of our God **shall** stand **forever.**"*
Isaiah 40:8

THEN . . . How do you **know** that He wasn't lying when He said...

"He that believeth on the Son hath everlasting life. . ." John 3:36

89

IF God doesn't have the power to preserve His Word for us perfectly, like He promised . . .

THEN . . . What makes you think that He has the power to save men's souls from everlasting fire????

"Much more then, being now justified by his blood, we shall be saved from wrath through him." Romans 5:9

IF . . . God doesn't have the power to keep His promises . . .
THEN. . . What makes you think that He has the power to change lives?

"Therefore if any man be in Christ, he is a new creature: old things are passed away; behold all things are become new." II Cor. 5:17

IF . . . God doesn't have the power to keep His Word . . .
THEN . . . what makes you think that He can give you **power** in your preaching?????

*"For the **preaching** of the cross is to them that perish foolishness; but unto us which are saved it is the **power** of God."*

Being a preacher is a great honor . . .

*"But thou, **O man of God,** flee these things; and follow after righteousness, godliness, faith, love, patience, meekness."* I Tim. 6:11

. . . BUT, it is also a grave responsibility!

*"**Woe** be unto the pastors that destroy and scatter the sheep of my pasture! saith the LORD."*
Jeremiah 23:1

If you don't believe that the Word of God is true and perfect, like God promised to preserve it . . .

*"The words of the LORD are pure words . . . Thou shalt **keep** them, O LORD, thou shalt **preserve** them from this generation for ever."* Psalm 12:6-7

THEN YOU HAVE ABSOLUTELY
***NO* BUSINESS BEING IN**
THE MINISTRY!!!

NO BETTER BIBLE?

A new minister came to a certain church. He was full of sophisticated knowledge and taught little from the Bible. At the end of two years he was told that one of the leading men of his church was ill. He went to see him. There was no chance of recovery; the man was dying. After a little talk the minister said, "Shall I read to you and pray with you?"

"Yes," replied the man, and beckoned to his wife to bring the Bible. A Bible was brought, and the minister opened it and saw a strange sight. Some books were taken out of it, some pages were torn away, some chapters gone, and some verses cut out; it was a shamefully mangled Bible.

The minister said, "Have you got no better Bible than this?"

The dying man said, "When you came to our church I had a whole Bible. But as soon as you told me that one book was fiction I tore it out; and that one chapter was not true, I removed it; and that some verses were unauthentic, I cut them out. And if I had had another year under you, I think I should have had the two covers, and nothing else."

CONCLUSION

"But there were false prophets also among the people, even as there shall be false teachers among you, who privily shall bring in damnable heresies, even denying the Lord that bought them, and bring upon themselves swift destruction.

And many shall follow their pernicious ways; by reason of whom the way of truth shall be evil spoken of.

And through covetousness shall they with feigned words make merchandise of you: whose judgment now of a long time lingereth not, and their damnation slumbereth not." II Peter 2:1-3

". . . even as there shall be false teachers . . ." (Westcott and Hort)

". . . who privily shall bring in . . ." (the revision committee of 1881 met in **private** for **10** years)

". . . damnable heresies . . ." (teaching salvation by works)

". . . even denying the Lord that bought them . . ." (**denying** the Deity of Christ, the virgin birth, the atonement.)

". . . and many shall follow . . ." (Look around . . . **Many** follow the modern versions)

". . . their pernicious ways . . ." (It's **dangerous** to deny the perfect Word of God)

". . . of whom the way of truth shall be evil spoken of . . . (The RSV preface says, "the King James has **grave errors**")

". . . and through covetousness . . ." (copyrighting "their" Bibles so **only they** can make money off them)

". . . they with feigned words . . ." (feigned means "to **imitate** so as to deceive" Standard Encyclopedic Dictionary page 233) *". . . make merchandise of you . . ."* (They're **using** you)

". . . and their damnation slumbereth not . . ." (To say the least, God isn't pleased with men tampering with and corrupting His Word.)

We **do** have God's Holy Word today! It **is** perfect and without error! If you can't believe that, then you are calling God a liar, and you will have to answer to Him for it!

> *"The law of the LORD is **perfect**, converting the soul: the testimony of the LORD is **sure**, making wise the simple. The statutes of the LORD are **right**, rejoicing the heart: the commandment of the LORD is **pure**, enlightening the eyes. The fear of the LORD is **clean**, enduring forever. The judgments of the LORD are **true** and **righteous** altogether."*
> Psalm 19:7-9

FOR MORE INFORMATION . . .

REFERENCES

"Which Bible?" . . . . by David Otis Fuller

"God Wrote Only One Bible" . . . . by Jasper James Ray

"The King James Version Defended" . . . . by Edward F. Hills

"Christian's Handbook of
  Manuscript Evidence" . . . . by Peter Ruckman

"Satan's Masterpiece - The New ASV" . . . . . by Peter S. Ruckman

"Counterfeit or Genuine?" . . . . by David Otis Fuller

"True or False?" . . . . by David Otis Fuller

"Believing Bible Study" . . . . by Edward F. Hills